T0040491

THE

WINTER

SLEEP

OF

CAPTAIN

LEMASS

THE
WINTER
SLEEP
OF
CAPTAIN
LEMASS
/
HARRY
CLIFTON

WAKE FOREST UNIVERSITY PRESS

First North American edition published 2012

Copyright © 2012 by Harry Clifton

All rights reserved. No part of this book may be
reproduced in any form, electronic or mechanical,
without written permission of the publisher
and author. For permission, write to:

Wake Forest University Press

Post Office Box 7333

Winston-Salem, NC 27109

Printed on acid-free, recycled paper
in the United States of America

LCCN 2012930964

ISBN 978-1-930630-60-4

Design by Quemadura

Cover and interior photographs:
Father and son on a mountain road to nowhere,
by David H. Davison / Davison & Associates

Wake Forest University Press

www.wfu.edu/wfupress

SIX COUNTIES

ELSEWHERE

THE
WINTER
SLEEP
OF
CAPTAIN
LEMASS

Dublin under sea-fog, dreeping weather,
Salt air blown inland ... The cab turns west
At Brady's pharmacy, into the nightlit drizzle
Of Harrington Street. And now for the acid test—
Alive to the danger, in this monkey-puzzle
Of ancestry, this maze of one-way streets,
Are you not scared, young man, of your Daddy's ghost
And his before him, waiting here to greet you,
Latest of blow-ins, ready to try again?
Is this where you get off, where the heart still melts
For the millionth time, old snow becoming rain
Off the Irish Sea—a flat in the Jewish quarter?
Immerse yourself, disturb the human silt,
An anchor feeling for bottom, in home waters.

TWENTY-SIX COUNTIES

LITTLE JERUSALEM

If you have to live somewhere
And you do, consider this
By streetlight, leaning drunk
Or just walking
Alone, through damp October,
An odour of bread-sticks on the air
And Gentiles, with the eyes
Of diamond-cutters, in the light
Of screen and anglepoise
Working late, the sabbath-breakers—
Everyone now an Israelite
Far from home, in the turfsmoke
Of old, converted terraces,
Coldwater streets, a tram
In the distance, a fin-de-siecle sigh
If I forget thee, O Jerusalem

Let the ruins of religion be my dwelling-place
Where echoing flights of stairs
At the clearing of a throat, in deep liturgical space,

Are answered by silence. And I climb, an apostate,
A worshipper of skylights, inheritor
Of cubic space, square feet, deconsecration,

Through latter days, Creation and Apocalypse,
To a rented halfway house
The key of simony opens, in chancel or apse.

High in the choirloft, light-motes, angels move
On the firmament of a ceiling. Listen—
A white noise of bathwater running, after love,

And voices, at the hour of vespers, smells of food,
The human returning. . . . Horae Canonicae—
Can I not find them beautiful and good,

So strangely lit, in this desecrated temple
Everyone shares, my pause on the stair
A secular prayer?
                    If I forget thee, O Jerusalem

Let me not be granted entry
To my homeland. Let me awaken,
A wandering Jew, in a faraway place
That is not America,
That must be some mistake,

And the grey realisation —
Ireland. . . . the beadle
Chanting psalms on Walworth Road
Where the synagogue takes root
In a feast of passion fruit—

The circumciser, blood on his hands,
And the Chrysler fleet
Asher rents, for funerals and weddings.
Beila boning kosher meat, and Harry
The Chagall of Stamer Street—

And the cards, the snooker,
The long afternoons of boredom
And orthodoxy, falling away
Like a quorum, to deaths, to goings away,
Imaginary Israels

I come back from, getting off
A bright new tram, at the heart of town,
To this, the latest station
The soul mistakes for its own —
Bell-clang, the broken trance

Of remembrance, in a maze
Of redbrick streets and holy days
Sold to the devil, my new address
The ruins of a church
And forty years in the wilderness.

A SON! A SON!

You around whom, at every hour,
The void thickens like an atmosphere
Rank with unsolved mystery, childish fears,

Go back now, through the Dublin lanes
To that very first year
Of malt and drayhorse, Francis Street, the Coombe.

Two women wait, in an ante-room.
A man who has crashed the lights
At Cuffe Street in the small hours, in the rain,

Chainsmokes endlessly—Players cigarettes.
Doctor Kidney, hedging his bets
And slapping nurses' bottoms, flashes through

In a white housecoat, the local deity.
Yes, we must all be patient,
Even you, in the ageless womb,

In the shadow of Saint Nicholas of Myra,
Where salt waits, oil in its cruse.
You will find your own way out of this maze

Of headscarves, factory whistles, cheap red meat
And dark soutanes on Thomas Street—
The fifties . . . Then as now,

To be hung upside down, on a brilliant scales,
A thumbprint on your brow,
Is all you know. And the old wives' tales

In the ante-room, the man dissolving in tears
Who has just become your father,
Lost in a fog of years.

THE EARLY HOUSES

FOR BELINDA MCKEON

They're all strung out, our alcoholic brethren,
On an infinite chain of early-morning drinks
In joints like this one. Little grey people
Unlike you, though—people without a future,

Dapper folk, with nothing to say for themselves,
The daily chemical hit, not ecstasy,
What they are after. Not exactly one of them
Myself, but the degree of separation

Less by the year, I can barely stay awake
As Smithfield market dawns, on a last blind date
Between night and morning, early and late—
The forklift whiz and rumble on the ramps,

The Chinese hauliers, their tailboards down
For the weight of the world. Little Britain Street,

North King Street—haunts of the underdog
Who lives off scraps, returns to his age-old vomit . . .

One last glance, before we break away
Into past and future. . . . Drizzle, dark before dawn,
The lights kept low, in deference to the wishes
Of the damned, in this strobe-lit gin-palace

Afternoon whites out, when the children come
To fling themselves at ecstasy, as I did myself,
And the binges start. For your company, much thanks,
In the underworld. *Slán*, and don't look back.

THE CRYSTALLINE HEAVEN

The new people, the quick money
Dante's Inferno 16.73

I sit up here, in the crystalline heaven,
 High as Dante, looking down
On the dog-eat-dog of Florence, Dublin town,
Through the marvellous dome of glass above Dail Eireann.
Coffee is over; a quarter past eleven
And the deputies file back in. Concentric hells
Of seats are filling up, conspiratorial,
Till the banging of the gavel, the Ceann Comhairle
Shouting for order, and then the division bells.

As suddenly, the House empties, through its backstage doors.
 Charlie Haughey crosses the floor,
Engages a woman I know in conversation—
Still beautiful, still a gazelle. After how many years
Of marriage to a Dublin auctioneer?
Above, the forces that govern the universe,

Light, reason and love, a Dantean vision,
Stream through the windows. I am alone up here
In the public gallery, as mid-morning disperses

Its scattered attendance, snoozing, as if not there,
    Through the luminous room.
My minister rises. I fold my *Irish Times*
And watch O'Snodaigh, leprechaun and elf,
Nervously scrape the three remaining hairs
Across his bald patch — him, my immediate boss! —
The prompter through the stage door of 'Whereas . . .'
A minor civil servant, like myself,
A lifer, splitting hairs till the crack of doom.

And darkly think to myself 'Inadequate
    For the business of state,
A Johnny-come-Lately . . .' Afterwards, in the lobby,
Hearing him talk, relaxing over a fag,
'Let Charlie soon starting shiting golden eggs
Or the country's fucked —' I'll know myself a snob,
A shadow of Dante, the chip on my shoulder,
Disinheritance, crystallising to heaven
High and light as the dome above Dail Eireann,
Sitting in judgement on Dublin, and getting older.

THE KEEPER OF SWANS

The night swans dibble in cold fluorescence,
Yellow sodium light. Is there no-one now,

With so much bread already cast on the water?
Yes, they were very kind to me, the ladies—

Look what became of them . . . Haunches, belly, breast—
Flashes of beauty, in an evil light

Their graceful necks dip through, to the nutrient ground,
And come up dripping. Let them sleep now,

Headless shapes afloat in their night-clothes
Where his own head swims. Is he sitting there,

The keeper of swans, or renegotiating
Eros and Death, the contract spelt in water

Tagging his whoopers, sending them back to haunt him
Every autumn, setting him free each spring?

CITRUS

All lemons are green to begin with, all oranges.
Ours, the nurslings of grey Irish light,
Turn yellow in winter. Meanwhile, through October,

In the tall windows, higher than human height,
Incarnate joy, against the logic of seasons,
Goes on ripening. Slowly a solstice approaches,

Drenched in cold moonshine, when the little tree
Self-pollinating, like a private mystery
Kept behind glass, from a collapsing world,

Goes south in itself, beyond poverty and death,
To infinite yellowness. . . .
                                    They are selling it
Already, on the Sicilian squares,

For less than nothing, as the sun moves up
Through the latitudes now, to catch us unawares
At the back end of January, still waiting,

In the days that never rise above themselves,
To slice it for its zest, against the grain
Of whisky, the false lift of gin and tonic.

STEPPENWOLF

Open that book on any page.
Out it spills, like one dead leaf—
Yourself in middle age
On a blind date. Her disbelief,

Suspicion, as you speak
Of Harry and Hermine,
The lonely man in the boarding-house,
The hostess on the scene

In a world of smoke and mirrors
Calling time, last orders please,
Between the crush of a Dublin bar
And the bottomless sleaze

Of Weimar. . . . She would like,
She says, to be Haller's daemon.
Nevertheless, there is always the clock
And how it ticks for women.

As you watch, her hair unbraids,
A snake at her back
Uncoiling, to the long white shock
Of a toothless old maid

In a fairytale. 'Be not afraid
Of foxtrots, jazz and good-time girls.
The real world is the underworld.
There, *mein lieb*, we all get laid,

Intensity, ecstatic truth
Are everyone's, at little risk
But childlessness, slow death —
And anyway, the Ball is Masked

As I am now. . . .'
                    It was that night
You saw her, for the first and last time,
Vanishing, like second sight,
Through Irish rain and German autumn,

Promising she could always find you,
Harry Haller, in the book
From which, just yesterday, there shook
A dead leaf, to remind you.

GERMAN WAR DEAD,

GLENCREE CEMETERY

You were blown west, your wings were too light,
And suddenly the air-pocket
Eire, sucked you into a tailspin.

Neutral space, a loss of human pressure —
Burn-out or soft landing,
Someone would lope towards you, over the bog,

His innocence, like a child,
Trailing beside him. . . . *Beware of that man.*
He carries inside him death by inanition —

And the collapsible silk
Of parachutes, the war in the upper air,
The contested laws of heaven, were never his business.

There are twelve of you here, and much snow
At a thousand feet, in the folded wings
Of the European theatre, where time means nothing.

I look at your graves. I see my own name written.

DAFFODILS

I hunker down, and see the daffodils
At eye-level, with the light coming through them.

It has happened once before.
I am being born. There is yellow light,

Indefinable, but absolutely pure,
Irradiating everything—maybe a vein or two,

My mother's or my own, the yolk of an egg
Or a streak of red in a bloodshot eyeball—

Either way, the world in its primary state
Being given. Ever afterwards

Yellow is my colour. And it multiplies
Endlessly. But nothing is the same.

The spring comes in. Again it is making windows
Of itself, to be seen but not seen through.

THE PARK

Because anyone sitting still attracts desire,
Even this will not be given you, the park
In June, the silence of a bench at eleven o'clock

On a Monday morning, or four on a Thursday afternoon.
Someone will drift towards you, unattached
And lonely. The spell will be broken, the wrong word said.

It is cool, but there is no death in the few token leaves
That must have come down last night, in the rain that freshened,
The tree-smell that remains. For this season there is no name,

Not summer, and none of the months of the year—
A something inside you. Search your mind
For the green arboriferous Word the boys and girls swing out of

Like a tree, and the lovers
On the grass in tantric mode, in an ecstasy
Of untouching, and the human buddhas, legs infolded, reading.

Branches, sheer translucent leaves—
You would die to get under them forever, if it were given you,
The park, on this, a day like any other day,

And not the knowledge of everyone ever met
Who will come upon you, sooner or later,
If only you stay here. No, not people, or the walkways

Made in another century, or the murmur of the great city
Everywhere in the distance, but this breathing-space
Where the void no longer terrible

But to be relaxed in, the depressions
Which anyway here are mild, incoming from the west,
Slow-acting, chronic, lifelong not acute

Are there to be sat through, waited out
On a damp bench, as a man sweeps up around you
And the sun comes out in real time, stealing over the ground.

BIRR

1

In the beginning was the Word
Or call it Birr, a little midland town
In the street-lit small hours, the rain sheeting down
And the drunken laughter of girls

With a moral age of centuries, who know it all
And do it darkly, under the castle wall.
The falconer sleeps. The whiskey burns on the water.
Again I would take you, stray daughter

Of the Shannon callows, in that strange pre-Raphaelite room,
The four-poster creaking, the good witch
Listening below us, stroking her three hound bitches
As the clock ticks, in her empty womb —

And wake beyond history, barracks and local schism
To biscuits and sloe gin on the sideboard
Left for us, in the aftermath of liaison,
Embarrassed and restored.

2

Postmaster Trollope, stationed at Birr,
Grows bored, begins a novel.
Rain and turfsmoke. Big House. Hovels.
Men and women who never were.

O the freedom of imagination
In a garrison town!
From the rooftops, jackdaws gossip
Of strange couples, floating down

To breakfast late, in station rooms
Where the walls have ears.
His Lordship, playing with space and time,
Switches on the moon and stars

Of a model universe. God is dead—
The locals, of course, still swarm to church,
Sleep justly, die in bed.
And what of ourselves, as we emerge

So sleepily, on this latest page
Where Trollope and God
Have lost the plot? The narrowguage
Railway, trundling sods

Through the black heart of the midlands,
Runs out of steam, abandons us here
At the back end of empire, quietly glad
Of a walk-on part, as the market square

Lets up its shutters
One more time, on a makebelieve,
A storybook town, a dream unshattered
The morning after love.

A CROSSROADS

I was down there
In the midlands, waiting
Under slate-grey skies,
At a crossroads.

Aspens whispered,
Miles of wheat. Eared silences
Ripened, imperceptibly,
Towards I knew not what.

There was one abandoned house.
Someone had walked away
Forever. In a window
Reflected, I saw myself—

To break with the past,
To make it out
In any direction,
More than roads were needed,

More than years, or strength of will,
Or the salting away
Of passage-money, endlessly lost
In the wrong Americas. . . .

This was the no-country.
Soulmakings, sacred wells,
Placeless ground
Neither here nor there.

Knowing it, standing still
For once, invisible
To passing cars, at last
I was getting somewhere.

THE DOUBLE CHAIRS,

MOUNT MELLERAY

When the great door slams, on twenty years
Of marriage, and we collect ourselves,
Let's settle, like the holders of holy office
Before us, in the two great wooden chairs
At the head of a soundless nave,
Alone together.
                Speech is irrelevant,
Corridors, footsteps. All the noise of the world
Going on outside. The yard-work, field-work
In the long summer meadows, sloping away
From the Knockmealdowns, to the wrong infinity—
God, they say, exacting His revenge
On Sunday afternoon, for the neglect
Of Sunday morning, in the carsick boredom
Of children, the cooling blood
Between husbands, wives . . . Incline to me here
But only a little, for I know you well,

And listen for the knock of silence
Echoing, in the wooden depths of the heart—

Silence, after all the high church music,
(Tin Pan Alley in the kitchen, Ambient in bed),
All the refracted days, like stained-glass windows
Seen from the inside—yellows, blues and reds.
The clatter of feet on the afternoon stairs,
The chopping of garlic on wooden boards,
The speechless rustle of how many thousand pages
Being turned, before the great Lights Out
On epithalamion, exequy. . . .
                         Brethren, dearly beloved,
You who come and go, on either side
Of our walled-in silence, changing the flowers
On the altar, hurrying your children
Through the darkened corridors, the mountains of the Vee,
The married, the celibate, each a dream of the other,
Leave us here a moment. Let us be.

MARRIAGE

In the dim void bit by bit an old man and a child
Samuel Beckett, 'Worstward Ho'

I am becoming your father
And you, my daughter,
On our wandering through the world
Must hold my hand now,
Two black dots against the snow—
An old man, a little girl . . .

All this started long ago.
I was woken, from the bestial sleep
Of ego-hood, by a strange glow
Behind the bedroom door
Where heterae with unbound hair
Were the company I would keep.

A strange glow, and then the light
As the door swung open

And you stood there, at the dream-threshold,
Ready. No more than a child
In the eye of second sight,
But the strangeness, the wildness,

Inside you! Certificates
Meant nothing. Scholarship?
Forget it. But the double-weight
One suitcase each, of useless books,
Enough to keep us ill-equipped
For a lifetime—those, my dear, we took.

Mine was the black coat in the corner,
Old, like myself, before its time,
Yours the pinafore, convent hat
You never grew out of. Two slow learners
As the small hours chimed
In the depths of the hallway, we set out.

Since then, snowscapes. Wilderness
That takes to itself a dozen names
Of countries, and is always the same.
One day, you are my mother,
I your son. Another
With clouded specs, directionless,

You lean on me, as we stagger on.
Do you ever miss the old days,
Sometimes you ask me. The vie en rose?
Old prostitutes with garters, stays,
Young women's laddered hose?
You my mother, I your son,

You my daughter, I your father—
Darling, if they could see us now,
Two black dots against the snow,
Two fly-by-nights the morning after
Over the skyline, managing who knows how,
They would tell us where to go. . . .

STAVROGIN AND THE LAME GIRL

Years later, in childless old age,
She'd remember. Her strange complaint
That first autumn of married love,
His sullen reading, page by page —
The Possessed — by the kerosene stove
All winter. 'Be a saint

Or nothing' the priests had told him.
And slowly, body and soul,
They'd grown together. The halfwit,
Sister to Captain Lebyadkin,
And Nikolai, who had married her for a bet.
Nothing, not even the catkins

Tasselling branches, seeing in spring
Could equal that miracle summer, ten years long,
With the rumour-mongers
Silenced, and the immaculate face
Etched with suffering, spiritual hunger,
Unclouding out of shame, disgrace,

Between them, like a moon . . .
                                          A fist at the door—
Lebyadkin, drunk. Behind him a rabble,
The world. She'd sit there
Gazing, all her cards on the table
Splayed for patience, into her looking-glass—
And the stove, where he'd read *The Possessed*,

Grey ashes now. They were all dead.
The miraculous had happened, just that once.
Abstractedly, out of her wits,
She'd tear at the hunk of black bread
And go on living, to outwait
Her libertine, her prince.

OCTOBER

The big news around here is the fall of leaves
In Harrington Street and Synge Street,
Lying about in pockets, adrift at your feet
As you kick them away. The other news is the trees—
Their yellow, as I speak, is unbelievable,
Not that you need me to tell you. Everywhere
The house is falling down around our ears
And it's wonderful, in the dry, spicy air,
How quietly it happens. Close your eyes,
Don't think, just listen. Hear them fall, the years
We came towards each other, out of a sun
Already westering. Look at us, even yet,
Exchanging tree-lore, twenty years on
In a leafless cathedral—bride and groom, well-met.

MISPRISION

There are mountains, only said to exist,
That have never yet come clear of their own mists

And shown themselves, as the philosophers say.
You come across them, driving east one day

From Limerick into Nenagh. Deep in your own lostness,
Swallowed between Silvermines, Rears Cross,

In a grey misprision. Word and thing
Ambiguous as signage. Blackbird on the wing

Stunned on your windscreen. Everything out of joint
Since 1922, when the disappointed

Landlord fled, and the circle of apples grew
At the base of his tree. For all you know

The creamery trucks are an ambush, the Black and Tans
Still drinking in the ghost of Milestone Inn,

And the barmaid, Erin's daughter,
Serving them, for a price, her pure well water,

Still with breasts to die for. . . .
                          Heightened country —
Headwaters blindly feeling for a sea

In any direction. Smell the Atlantic salt
And guess the valley, deep in an old earth-fault

Sleep at the wheel, between dying and being born,
Pay no-one allegiance, fake your returns

And dream of a day when everything comes clear
And the only real words are *I am here*.

DYING GENERATIONS

On such a day, with the future cancelled out,
We live in the present. I drive Desmond
To Limerick, for his hour of back massage,
And do the shopping. The old man
Looks after himself, potters about
In the kitchen, though his mind is gone
And the mess of broken meat is there on the table
When I get back. The gardener has been
With the transplants. Somebody found
An odd bird down by the river
Where Desmond opened a path, between his fields
Of wheat and potato.
                                    On such a day
Who wouldn't feel, when the mist is everywhere,
Serotonin drops, of mood into light,
Are the one solution? My skull
Was thin at birth. I sense the oncoming fronts
From the Atlantic, days before they reach us
Deep inland. A great ache

Or is it the change, or the slow beginning
Of something inherited, as the old man
Goes to pieces? I no longer believe in anything
But the greenness, the greyness,
The eternal everydayness
Of Ireland. Time, they tell me, will come back—
The past, the future. Meanwhile I wake
With an empty mind, to a high ceiling,
A jug of clear spring water,
The buzz of a chainsaw, somebody felling a tree.

THE REBEL TITANS

In the Black Valley, radio silence —
Eros disconnected, dead,
In mizzling rain, a white noise of headwaters.
Where could I go from here, to rouse the daughters

Of Mnemosyne, from apathy,
Melancholia? In the Silvermines
Gone saturnine, in their massy chains of ore,
The Rebel Titans lay, unable to roar.

Typhon and Dolor, Atlas and the Gorgons —
Loaded rifts of personal pain
And stolen thunder. North Tipperary Riding —
Somewhere in earshot, the Nenagh train . . .

Through the remains of the very first day
I was driving eastwards. Deep in Aherlow,
Its cave of pure acoustics,
Surely a god cast down

Might rise again? At last, I could try it out,
The cosmic interstellar shout
Of infinite joy inside me.
Tethys, Ops, Porphyrion, they would hide me,

Their adopted child, as the night came down
On the glottal watercourses'
Tiny tinkling, on the lights of Bansha town,
The paddocks, and the frightened horses.

SKELLIG MICHAEL

The 'vine transplanted out of Egypt'
Is, they tell me, Ireland.
I, who did my penance on the mainland,
Now look back
From a lost Atlantic rock

At all those towns named Dysart
Meaning 'desert'. Surely to Christ
They knew of us, the Fathers,
Way back then, in the Middle East—
Occluded in our weather,

Or call it a spirit-mist,
Where the selkies bark, the oceans break,
Invisible therefore real
As the books insist.
Eight miles back

Is Ireland, life, temptation,
Sloping green, through its stone-walled fields,
Its solid yellow farmsteads.

Too much milk and honey
The eremite said,

And yes, our crossing was wild
In a blown spume
Of backwash, diesel fumes,
As the sick-bucket's stomach-trash
Went over with a splash

And the croaked-up devils
Spat themselves out
And the world turned medieval.
Beehive huts, on their high redoubt,
(They grew their own evil)

And the six-hundred-odd steps
Of slabbed atonement
To get there ...
                No, as the engine stops
And the pilgrims stuffed with Quells
In the oily swell,

The guilty, the inadequate,
Each with a middle-aged dread,
Are lifted up, and gently swung ashore,
I feel I have been here, in my head,
Too many times before.

THE YEAR OF THE YELLOW MEAL

1

Drifting out of the north,
We shipped oars
Inboard, went with the force.

Drifting out of the west,
Eternal unrest—
Ebb and flow, our whole existence . . .

East and south, we kept ashore
On the island. Time passed
Without landfall, though the land was there

Across the strait, immense, unreal—
Ireland. There we would go
In Sunday clothes to drink and deal.

2

A stony world, of treelessness and sea-light
Open to nothing—call it heroic.
If we were Greek, you might think of us as stoics.

As it was, a priest arrived twice yearly,
A boatload of bluecoats,
Guns at the ready, drumming up rent arrears.

I held it myself, one end of a measuring-chain
That stretched, through drystone wall
And gable end, to the courts of claim and counter-claim. . . .

We could make a god of anything. Black kelp
For the fields, a bullock washed ashore
That fed us for months, without His Majesty's help—

The Teeraght flash, "last light before America,"
World War salvagings, sea-metals, fire to steal
In the year of the yellow meal.

3

That year, starvation,
Our theology, put us in
At the weedgrown quays
Of Ventry and Dunquin.

There was such a thing as time.
It hung from a chain
On a merchant's waistcoat.
Out of Kingdom Come

We had drifted. This was amazing!
Could a chanceless world
Exist? Manpower raised
To godhead, beyond heaven or earth?

Meal and flour, the sacks went down
To the leaking hold
And dampened, soon to moulder.
Off we went on the town—

A few lights, thrown together,
Call it Metropolis. One steep street,
Enough to be lost in
Forever, on bare feet . . .

People, you see, without a nation,
Only a gut metaphysics
Bilge-pumped to infinity
On a leaking vessel

Fleeing westward, Irish Greeks,
For whom the word *sea*
Meant nothing, who could only speak
Of blind force, necessity.

RAKESTREET

Would you believe it, I got lost again
And all roads led to Rakestreet. Which was which,
The short road or the long? A girl of ten
Behind her counter, drew me a thumbnail sketch

Of space in time. The Big House was, she said,
Five minutes away, or seven hundred years.
Nephin, nebulous in its hat of cloud,
A reference point. I would never get out of here

Until I fell in love with my condition—
Rakestreet, with its boy behind the bar,
Its sweatshop, and its permanent television
In the background, rumbling from afar

Of war and worldly sex, greed and ambition,
While the dead slept under lichened stone
Behind Kilmurry chapel. Older than religion,
Older than history, this quiet need to atone

By staying local, once at the very least,
For an hour, a day, a lifetime. Marry the girl,
Buy up the stock, become one with the deceased —
Let Crossmolina and the Big House world

Be damned to its own eternity, Lough Conn
Forever signalled, never come upon,
Lose itself, like the reason I came
In the first place, and my aboriginal name.

THE POETS RETURNING

Back they have come, to hold court
In their old bohemia. Wisely, the City State
Leaves open a coffeeshop, a limelit bar,
A house or two of ill resort—
For Eros, it knows, can never integrate.

Their women, driving them deep into the mountains,
Watch as the wild birds flock to their feet,
In love with innocence. Did they never grow up
Through power and corruption,
Undeclared global war, the law of the street,

And all their lifetimes in that separate dimension,
Exile? There they are
Like revenants, old now in the cocktail hour,
The notes of a lounge piano. So many years—
The hostesses no longer pay attention,

The muses are shrewder and the coinages all changed.
The gold, the silver and bronze—
Each seeks its level, in the scheme of things.
Slave-owners, favourite sons
Rule over everyone, like philosopher-kings.

A million headlights stream against the windscreens
Of the taxis taking them home—
Lonely for Eros, as the state evolves,
Doomed to repeat themselves
In a new republic, neither Greece nor Rome.

THE WINTER SLEEP

OF CAPTAIN LEMASS

1923

The life of the country
Hardened against you
Like frost, and a new front

Opened — brother against brother,
Choice against choice,
Disputing the high ground. Your eyes,

Blindfolded, beheld the ideal State
As the real one steadied itself
To annihilate you.

How to survive it, the force of exclusion,
The freezing out of the soul
At the site of its own execution?

In the high cold, in the light snow
Of the Dublin mountains, a fox
Made its own tracks

And vanished. . . .
                                    A single shot—
A hundred years of travelling echoes,
Family history, unmarked plots.

1943

'Harry' she said, 'it might have been Marlborough Street—
Or was it Griffith barracks? Anyway, I had the Irish
And typed for De Valera, battering memos out

On a civil service Remington, not caring or having a clue
What any of it meant (two regulars
Guarded his office) but simply admiring the view

Of the Dublin mountains, through those wonderful high windows
We inherited from the British. The War,
As I remember, had entered its second-last winter—

Joseph gathered firewood in the Phoenix Park
And Charlie cycled to the Featherbed
To cut turf, singing arias from the D'Oyly Carte . . .'

The snow is off the mountain. Griffith, McKee—
Limp tricolours, the barrack-light of Sparta,
Men and women in battle fatigues, against an invisible enemy.

'. . . Joseph a suicide, Charlie without position
In the new republic . . .'
                              Go on speaking. Shed a little more light,
If anyone will, on our bitterness, our confusion.

                              2004

        It's always cold up here
        Even now, in summer. The Featherbed
        Older, without knowing it, by a hundred years,
        A book for a pillow, under my head,

        A splinter of ice in the soul
        Still growing. Infinite winter
        Hides the fox in his den,
        Obliterates the entrance

With butts and bottletops, used french letters,
The fugitive night-pleasures
Of the republic . . . Elders and betters,
Charlie, Joseph, Noel Lemass—

When will you ever go to ground?
Must I lie here endlessly, wait
For the whole of the Dublin mountains
To move, and the City State

At last to stand clear, a dazzle of lights
Forever stretching westward?
Groggy with nature, history, space,
Again I kiss myself goodnight

In the name of the lost, the disinherited,
All who never came back from the dead
To tell their story, claim their place—
And sink back into the Featherbed

By a memory-stone, a fouled lair,
Bog-cotton whispering in my ears,
The sound of a car, a light somewhere
In the silences, the years.

SIX COUNTIES

SWEAT-HOUSE

1

Someone let the fire go out
Around here, in the eighteenth century.

Ever since, in the damp country
Of snails and mushrooms

You come back to, for another summer
Of wild garlic and swimming,

The balm and incense
Of pine-needles under your feet,

Something is missing, something is incomplete.

2

A rattle of planks on the backboard of a lorry
Far below, and the drone of a harvester
Float up here, as you sweat it out

Stark naked, under a wind-bitten scarp
At the far end of summer.
Any minute now, he will happen by

In the shape of a cloudmass, or a butterfly—
The Evil Spirit, forever whispering
To the demoralised 'You are better than any of this. . . .'

Bending your ear, with talk of the wretched half-lives
Of the townlands, the abandoned houses,
Trees of human twistedness grown up through them . . .

Cleg and grasshopper, creatures of heat and thunder,
Sting and fiddle. A green Gethsemane
Accomplishes itself, the master-plan for humanity

Out of which climbs one couple . . . Quick, get dressed
And make yourself scarce, before they get to you
Trespassing here, in the love-nest.

3

Crawl back in, if still you can,
Through the low door
Of humility, to a flagged floor

Where, centuries back,
Someone lit a fire once
In the realm of innocence,

Doused the smouldering bracken,
Stoked up steam.
How many souls could they cram

In there, shoulder to shoulder,
Badgers in a sett
Reeking, feeling the sweat

Leach out of them like pain
Or an act of atonement?
The lintel of stone,

The plunge-pool
Just outside, and afterwards
Resumption, the dank wool

Of homespuns, going home
To eternal winter . . .
Traumatised, de-centred,

Leaving the car-door open,
Crossing the fields,
What on earth do you hope for,

You, from the loneliest century?
To such a womb, my friend,
There is no re-entry.

AT THE CROSSKEYS

What are you doing up here, young man,
In the high country, behind Lough Neagh,
Where the pub, according to plan,
Burned down for the insurance pay?

Whitewash, and a gravelled yard,
The same folk history on the walls,
And the barmaid—singed blonde hair—
Proof that it happened, after all.

Bathed in their own reflected glory,
Men are drinking. Slow time
The colour of Jameson, Jim Beam,
Drips from the optics. Where is history

Now, as the harvesters drone
Outside, and the wheel of the seasons
After midnight, spins out blizzards of chaff
In the *son-et-lumière* fields of June?

How did they live it, the sheet of flame
Each passed through, without moving,
Without speaking? Someone would cover it,
They knew, somebody settle the claim—

And the quality of their silence
Alone, might modify
One eyeblink, as they waited to die
In this hitching-post, on the high cold miles,

Belfast to Derry, their conflagration
Behind them, their horses still to be fed
Or changed—that hames on the wall—
For the unforeseeable country ahead.

A SWALLOW

You can't manufacture a swallow—
Try as you might, it will dip and weave
All summer, through the space
Between word and thing.

Where nothing is forced,
Where everything is itself,
Not even the cat, with whom you share
A predatory will, gets closer.

Stone is one thing, stonechat another.
Yeats's Rough Beast, Blake's Tyger,
Made as they are from will and language,
Slouch, but never approach it.

There they go, July and August—
The slow months here
For sitting still, for stalking yourself
To a moment of unawareness,

Self-surrender, when the grass invades you,
The swallows fly right through you,
And the yard itself, a proto-space
Anticipating language, waits for September

To declare open season
On the absconded, the barn to yawn
And the abandoned air to fill again
With shots, with moral pressure.

THE JUST

It was a wild summer, up there in the country
With the rain coming down
All August, the crops flattened in the fields
And a mad whisper in the eaves
That would feel comforting
If you were ready to die, and the business of life
Concluded, successfully or not—
Condensed to a drop, in the silence between gusts,
The silence of the just,
With a roof above you, a few rooms
To dispose yourself in, to leave as a legacy,
Nothing more. And the autumn
You might not live to see, already around you
In the fields, unharvested,
Overripe, with the unimaginable future.

DEEP ULSTER

It was here, the elemental centre,
All the time. Eternally present, repeating itself
Like seasons, where the times and dates
For swallows and household fires are written down,

The grouse are counted, the quotas of stocked rainbows.
All that love of order, for its own sake.
Only the hill-farms, and the high sheep country
Above politics—the enormous relief

Up there, as the dialect names of skies
Return, along with their clouds, and the old knowledge
Opens the mind again. To dream, to just potter
In the yard, to fiddle with local stations

In the kitchen, where news that is no news
Finally, at last, fills up the years
With pure existence. Lit from beneath
The fields are evenings long, the tree by the house

Where Vladimir and Estragon kept vigil
With the stillness of commando and insurgent
Frightens no-one. Slow through the air
A heron, shouldering aside the weight of the world,

Is making for its colonies, coevals
In a state plantation. . . .
                              Nowhere but here
In the high right hand of Ireland, do the weather-fronts
Give way so slowly, to such ambivalent light.

A MIST OFF THE LOUGH

You alone saw through it,
Local weather, into the truth of a world

Where everything in its first, original version
Huge, Platonic, stood around and waited

For a child to name it. Your days
Were so small, so tiny your word-hoard

Piled like winter feed at the end of the yard.
In the mornings, a pheasant might appear,

A neighbour's cow, a fish dropped out of the air
By a passing heron. Water, sky,

The whole wide field of vision
Occluded, untranslateable—

The badger-cries in the lane all night
At mating-time, the creak of mattress and head-board

Somewhere about the house, as you tried not to hear
From the den of writing, turned up the heat

In the shifting crystalline dank ionosphere
Of never-to-be-clarified years.

FELON

It was deep in a small wood,
Autumn, when I came upon him
Out of my own late life.

He was weighing his prospects
As I had done — a fowling-piece
Under arm, a pocketful of bird-shot,

A litter of spent cartridges
At his feet. A changeling
At the dangerous age

Of felony, transportation,
Draped in a camouflage jacket,
Mottled in light and shadow.

Already, there would be women,
Drink, unlicensed cars
And trespass at all hours.

I would deliver him, at a stroke,
From October, local skies,
The old life of instinct.

Trials would follow. Redemption
In the punishing light
Of the tropics. I saw it all

Already, through a glassy screen
Of dripping haws, as he lowered his gun —
My real, my illegitimate son.

AT TOOME

There was a pheasant somewhere around,
Croaking; drowned out
By the small birds
Nearer. Would it enter the yard
And dazzle us, or be lost
In the morning, in the wet fields
Levelling out amazement?

A door was opened, a comment made.
Somebody flung a bucket of slops
Across the air. In the silence
New and frightened,
Finches, tits, the little birds,
An army helicopter heard,
Moved in, to their feeding-grounds.

AN UNDERSTANDING

This, I believe, is called walking out with someone.
Limitless water on one side. On the other

Long stone farmsteads, where, for generations,
People have made their beds and lain on them,

Afterwards giving birth to the likes of ourselves
Going forth again in silence, the wide world watching—

A city-slicker, still with the crease in his pants,
A local girl, above the tongue of scandal,

Only the years ahead of us, like an aisle
Mute with witnesses—briar and thorn,

The eyes and ears of the place, the summer breeze
Inrushing, flattening bodice, breast

Of a centuries-old dress
Against your body, as the headland thins

To now or never, and I take your hand.
This, I believe, is called reaching an understanding.

TOOME

At the lowering of the boom,
The letting-through of water
From the lough—a slow pour
So long ago, so much past behind it—
I happened into Toome. . . .

The place of an ancient ford.
There must always have been people,
Commerce, where the hauliers
Changed gear, and the girders shook
Beneath me. On they would go
To whatever the future held.

A little girl, who once was you—
The same bangs and plaited hair—
Skipped, in her pinafore,
Over the main street. O my love
I could have been anyone
Taking a road, for right or wrong,
Through a strange, forgettable town,

But the water turned to sky
And the sluice-gates opened,
Time stood still. . . .
                    Somewhere
The sea makes nothing of all this—
But not yet. We are not there yet.
Instead, the rattle of haulage,
The passings-through, the dailiness
Of the main street, and a man
Transfixed, on the bridge,
Who stopped once, and stayed forever.

SOFT WATER

We have a rainbarrel now,
New guttering. On average days
A trickle-down effect,
But always accumulation.

Today, a wind from the west.
Our blurred self-images
Swim together, drifted through
By the death of leaf and spider.

Soft, untreated water,
Pure, undrinkable.
And the green-fingered
Like yourself—no lead, no fluoride—

Keeping your looks forever,
Its priestesses ... For the hands,
For the hair thrown forward
Over your head, as you kneel

To the basin's shallow element,
Worshipping the everyday.
Nothing can measure that downpour.
Multitudes haul it away.

THE EEL

In the crowded yard, in the oily blue smoke
Of an eel supper, the eel looks on.

He is home for the summer. She is home for the summer,
Metamorphosing, the one in the other,

Androgynous, ambivalent, slipping in and out
Of the local, the universal,

Reading about itself, in the Book of the Eel,
As a disappearing species,

Toying with its own myths, renewing its passports,
Wondering whether or not a child is possible,

Longing, unconsciously, for autumn
As the tractor roars all night, and the pilot-lights flash

In the fields outside. For the night-phosphorescence
Of cities, the lifelong shedding of skins.

THE SECOND MOWING

Occupied with things beyond himself,
A man is making a huge circle. The second mowing

Well under way, the windrows upon windrows,
Black scatterings of crows, ahead of the rotary blades,

Making their own hay. And the narrowing drone
As the centre is approached, unconsciously.

Who will overtake it, him or me?
For a moment, sound is lost. Then back it comes,

The tractor, from the end of the long acre,
Riding its soundwave . . . I am just a window

In the distance, a winking pane of glass
At the edge of the work, my openings, my closings

Immaterial to the bite of the mighty tyre-treads
Into the terrestrial, as the pattern appears.

FALSE MERIDIAN

I was, as usual, missing the point.
The sound of a hot-press door
Being shut, the slow clump
All day, up and down stairs,
Were what they were actually living for,

The women of the house,
Who set up poles, unwittingly
Or not, for their drying-lines,
On a false meridian,
North to South, between two times,

The daily, the eternal.
On their knees, it would appear,
To nothingness, as the ashes were cleared
From the grate, and I hung back, yards away,
Watching, from another world. . . .

Each of us playing to our strengths,
Silent, not unfriendly,

Over meals, the weather our common ground,
Each of us going to fantastic lengths
In the name of the real

As the years closed in, and we drew together
Over boardgames, or cards,
And the great throwback began
Past their activities, and my words,
To a simple world again.

PIPISTRELLE

At no point, in the whole of that northern night,
Was there total eclipse of light,

Only a yellow streak, low down in the sky
Against which little squeaks, subliminal cries

Would dash themselves, so to speak—
The pipistrelles. Hours later, dawn would break

To the sound of illegitimate shots
In the field nearby. And whether or not

She had slept, in a strange bed at the end of the house,
One must have broken in, a flitter-mouse,

Ages ago, to winter behind her shelves,
Her married remnants. A piece of the dark, detaching itself

To circle the bare bulb, as wounded, afraid
As she was. Widowhood

And the eerie light of the midnight sun,
And silence, and the abandonment, one by one,

Of room after room, to a high soprano wail,
A purity off the scale

Of human reckoning, would bring it on—
Enlightenment, time to be gone.

THE CHANGE

1

You look out. A shock of green
Has colonised the yard.
Trees you never learned the names of
Have taken over. And the pines
In the garden have grown
To supernatural heights
Where they wave, still,
In the same south-westerlies.
Tell me, when did you blink
And all this happen?
How did we change, to this other woman,
This other man, walking abroad
Under great skies, pacing a flat field
By a lakeshore, feeling our years
As matter turns to spirit?

2

Before it all disappears, and the inner life
Takes over, lengthening like a shadow,
Remember the half-wild garden, gone to seed,
The gnarled red hawthorn, blazing in April,
Dead by August, a silvery disc
Suspended, shimmering, from its middle,
Scaring a few late birds from the berry feast.

The tree you grew from an acorn overtakes you
Into the future. Potato furrows,
Overgrown, are the mass graves of appetite
Dying for resurrection. A time that is not our time
Overtakes us, before and after
Birth and death, the disposition of lands.
Through the field-grass wind pours, ceaselessly.

Lodge it back in a tree-fork, the fallen nest
All cattle-hair, moss and twigs in a glaze of mud
Where the firstlings of imagination
Came of age. In a lost, external realm
The mother-bird watches. Yard by yard, we abandon it,
Hour by hour, the ground of natural love
As night comes on, and it's time to go inside.

3

In the bright scullery, silence.
Up in the kitchen
Salt, in a small glass cruet,

The crystallised afterlife
Of marriages and widowhoods
When the ducts run dry.

We take it with everything.
It drifts, like sediment
Into the bloodstream. Experience —

But that was never the point.
Doesn't it possess you
Now, on the creaking stairs,

That same dynastic urgency
As myself? Black doors
On a darkened landing,

Slivers of light under each.
There are women there
Foetal, reading late.

Cover my eyes, for Christ's sake
And ride me, one and all,
For life and the future, house and lands!

I stay too long in the bathroom.
You, in a clinical mirror,
Examine your breasts.

THE DESERTED WIFE

The rain, by now, is beating in from the west,
And you who are left, in that outlying house
At the end of generation, lean your head, as well you might,

On the cold of a windowpane, repeating
Like a mantra that has calmed them all there for centuries
That these days are the worst days

And this time it is true, there is no-one left to listen
Only the blowing outside, the dripping,
The cold reflections. No-one, least of all me,

For the realisation has finally dawned —
I am gone forever. Dead or asleep
In another body, hundreds of miles to the south,

At the start of another life. O child, for you were always a child,
How far ahead of me, on the way of death,
You find yourself faring now! There is no-one left,

And nothing but glass between your own high forehead
And the cries, that are all ancestral cries,
Of driven birds in a rain-slicked yard. Was it too far out,

The house on the foreshore? Nobody builds on water,
And the trees, the soul of the place,
Have taken it over. I hear them out there, even yet,

Their dark collective soughings, last thing before sleep—
And who could have the heart
To chop them down . . .
                              It has stopped, your long weeping—

Everything inside is eerily quiet,
The soundless clock in the kitchen,
The perfect yellow orchid, the prayerbook on the sill,

Everything that batters at eternity
Like sheer unbreakable glass.
You have closed the gap now, childhood into death—

There is nothing in between. A calmness, supernatural,
Outside time, where the words that reach you,
Uttered by the living, come from beyond the grave.

NORTH KOREA

Can I not build you a house in North Korea,
Fry you an eel in a heavy pan,
And pollan in season, off an inland sea
When our ship comes in? O my husband, O my man

Who failed in things the rest of the world understands —
Seventy miles to the north, as the crow flies
Through the battle-zones, is a never never land
Time forgot, where he who awakens dies. . . .

On the shakiest bed that anyone ever made love in,
Under a horsehair blanket, while we mate,
I will kick out your lights forever

And leave you asleep, through the grey and terrible years
Of No Surrender, Mongols at the Gates,
With the faintest sound of a fife and drum in your ears.

THE MAP OF BECOMING

There's nothing out there, only life and death.
The stuff in between that crowds the senses everywhere else
And gets in the way of emptiness and cold

Is blown away like smoke, as the grey Atlantic fronts
Move in, from the south-south-west,
And rattle the sheet-iron of the dipping-pens

High in the hills, and make of the water-table
An altar of surface sheen, in the clearing instant,
To sacrifice hope on, understand everything

Suddenly, as the hunter returns
With nothing on his belt, and the boy-fisherman
Caught between joy and loneliness, on an unfrequented shore,

Breaks sabbath. . . .
                    Land, sky and water
Meet out there at a point. Or call it the soul
On Sunday afternoon, at large in a space

To be lost in, where no-one wishes to be
And everyone, sooner or later,
Finds himself, on the map of his own becoming.

THE APPROACHES

A childless, futureless road
And then nothing . . . Is that it?
Or start believing in a God
Beyond the temporal limit

Of westering skies, wide, melancholy
Uncut fields and paced-out walls
As we drive towards it slowly,
The house that has us both in thrall.

They are gone now, the hours of light
It took to get here. Might-have-beens,
Lost wanderyears. But that's alright—
We are trading it in, the seen

For the experienced, the car-keys
For the end of the journey,
When distances have lost their power
And the heart beats slower

In tomorrow's cold, a coming weather
One degree north of yesterday.
High latitudes—as they say,
There is nothing up here

But wind and silence, passing clouds,
Light diminished half a tone,
A dish left out all night for the gods
By morning turned to stone.

So take a right, go down two gears
And stay in second, where the church is
And the pig-farm. Only the approaches
Are terrible, only the years,

The getting here, which takes forever.
Second selves, a barren crone
On a bicycle, a man alone,
They're waving. . . . It's now or never,

Ruin or the one true Rome—
The shape of a house
On the skyline, the release
Into childhood, and the coming home.

ELSEWHERE

CROSSING SWEDEN

Insistently, a foreign tongue
I can only interpret as Song
Comes over the air, as the train roars on.

Even as it speaks
Ice breaks, and fast-flowing rivers
Take over, the dazzle of lakes,

The shutter-speed of sun through trees
As the mind clicks into gear
And the eyes unfreeze.

A windfarm's slow propeller
Threshes cloudy skies—
I wonder who lives out there, who dies,

And see my own reflection
Rushing past, to the greater world
Of Stockholm Central, Gothenburg,

As the changes are announced
In that Scandinavian, singsong tone
I recognise now as my own.

It wants to be helpful, to be kind.
Abroad in the north country
Of my own mind,

I hear it—any tongue will do—
Interpreting the hinterland,
Seeing me through.

CHRISTIANIA

I see you, Christiania, in the light
Of Blake and Engels, other days
Than Copenhagen. From the abandoned looms
Like visionaries, the women have long since risen,
And the men have gone their ways
From an age of press-ganged war and debtors' prison.
For an instant, poised above time,
Being, not doing, is the real Jerusalem —

Strewn with industrial dreck and shipyard timber.
Somebody plinks out tunes
On a stolen piano. The walls are strip cartoons
Of freakonomics, war. And the artels sing
In the communal kitchen. Not that I ever remember,
Or the world was ever so young,
Or the mud of Pusher Street a Golden Age,
Coming, as I do, from over the bridge,

Dystopia, where the Lords of Misrule,
Born old and penny-wise,
Catch holy innocents, and drag them off to school.
They say whoever leaves you, Christiania, dies—
The laidback, the naïve,
Their hair down to their feet, like Adam and Eve,
Speaking if not in tongues, at least in Danish,
Dreaming Edens, as they vanish.

BETHEL

A clear light, at all hours,
A girl at reception. And the evangelised
Stepping heavenward, up the wooden stairs,
Each with his version of Christ,

Showing the world a clean pair of heels
For Bible, drying out and three square meals —
And you, who sank your lance in Moby Dick,
Blissed-out, broke, by the Skaggerak . . .

Nyhavn, Christianshavn
Mingling, splitting their crucified cabin-lights —
Oil on water. Rustbuckets
In from Greenland, off the north Atlantic route,

Stinking tubs from Rekyavik, the Faroes.
Was it only yesterday
She Saved you, by the warehouse
Of flensed whales — the unadulterated joy

Of the first woman in years
On your skin, an Ishmael giving thanks
For a few words of English, the lingua franca
Of the homeless everywhere,

Knowing Bethel, "heavenly place,"
Brought back to yourself, in the after-trance,
By women in lights along the quays,
A laying on of hands?

A CHINESE HARBOUR GIRL

Note: I invest you with no especial aura,
Though the work you do might well be termed divine—
Naked, only the latest in a line
Divested of myth, advancing towards me

In a spirit of frank and humorous exchange . . .
Not that I amn't dazzled—not by light,
I mean your body, the wave of excitement
At the dimming of the lamp, the heightening of strangeness—

Most certainly I am. . . . But the one dark instant
Neither short nor long, when the business between us
Is done, takes nothing away

From gantries, miles of quays and ships at anchor,
The whiff of commerce, the literal meaning
Of Chinese neon—tariffs, rates of pay.

MOTHER TONGUE

I came from gypsies, on my mother's side.
There would be dawns, in childhood,
When somebody strange came out of the night
To sit at table. Father smoked,
Said nothing. Mother, in a language
Not of this world, wept and harangued.
And the visitor just sat there
Listening. A little woman, glamorous
In the manner of half a century back,
Her perfume like a sounding-board for the senses
Now, at the time of writing . . .
                                    Barely awake
In the hour of stripped illusions, bitter words,
I drank the milk of origins like a godchild —
Lost hotels, a long pre-natal chain
Of wanderings . . . And this, our household lie
Eclipsed by electric light and shattering clarities,
Broken into. Shouts, recriminations,
Go *inside, we'll call you* . . . Through a wall

No-one breached for twenty years
I heard the taxi called. She came inside
And held me to her. *No-one here understands me —*
You alone, morcito . . .
                   Years would pass,
I would run away. It was out there somewhere,
The mother-tongue. By now she was striking camp
Or putting down new roots, in another town,
With an absolute stranger, who would educate me
In gambling, horses, family sagas
Endlessly added to, nowhere written down.

MATÉ-DRINKING

A door blows open, into a vanished world.
A woman sits there, *maté*-drinking,
Arucanian Indian — my grandmother.
One sip through her metal straw, then another,

And the level slowly sinking
In the gourd, as pure reality heightens.
'Enter child, there's no need to be frightened.
They married me off, you see. I was only a girl,

And falseness, lack of love, became my portion.
Here in the servant's quarters
Of Misiones, no-one uses the English delf.

I speak to you now, from the other side of war
And orphanhood. Child, be true to yourself. . . .'
(Mother reaches past me, slams that door).

LETTER FROM BUENOS AIRES

WITOLD GOMBROWICZ 1904–1969

Here it's Spring, at the other end of the earth —
The eucalypti seeding, and the plane-trees,
Onto the Avenida. Buenos Aires
Facing away from the sea, neither south nor north
Of anywhere real, abandoned by history,
A city of exile . . . *empanadas*, beer

At a sidewalk table. Who am I writing to?
Lena and Marisa, Andrea who flirts
Already, at fourteen — the lonely daughters
Of the *estancias*. Dominique du Roux,
Smieja, back in Europe, taking my books to heart.
The dryness in the air, the lime in the water —

Yesterday I saw my face in a mirror,
Lined already. . . . 'See that twelve year old?'
Frydman yells from his chessboard. 'Man of straw

I had her—I, a poet, above the law!'
Okay, okay. I have made my soul
At tables such as these, for too many years

Behind the Retiro, haunt of illicit loves,
Not to know such things must never be spoken of
In the salons of Ocampo, Bioy Casares.
Self-immortalised on a toilet wall,
My apologia 'Not being a shorthorn bull,
How could I hope for fame in Buenos Aires?'

Aim: to be cold and disciplined, where the will
Disintegrates, in this huge
Unpressurised vacuum, middle age,
Sown with pampas grass and one-horse towns,
Hotels out of season, rooms without pen
Or stationary, for there is nothing here to distil. . . .

Quilimbo, or Colimba, bringing me back to life
With rice and chicken. Goldberg, the master of chess
I lost to, in Santa Fe. Helena, my temporary wife
In Santiago del Estero. So the time passed—
Absolute time, the river of rivers, Parana—
Writing the empty essence of man,

Returning from the dead, to find myself famous,
Milosz, Jelenski, back in Paris,
Calling me home to Europe, where the ghosts are laid.
On the floor a million letters, in Venezuela Street,
To step back into, a man half-shade,
Half-revenant, my destiny half-complete.

THE RAIN SHADOW

All who got there
By dreaming or default,
Found themselves in a desert
Of crusted salt.

They called it Atacama,
Went to work. Across the divide
Of the Andes, Colonel Fawcett's rain
And stolen thunder. Dry-eyed,

Tearless, trying to speak,
Endlessly they cleared their throats
On this side of the puritan trek,
Emotionless, remote.

Father began to crack
In three weeks flat.
Pisco sours, and Indian women,
Friendly, bowler-hatted,

Chewing *coca*, drinking *maté*
Breathing the clearest air
Astronomy dreamed, religion craved—
The clarity of despair.

Mother, a girl so nice
In so nasty a place,
Kept vigil on the coastal plain,
Heard the tinkle of ingot trains

Nightly, into Antofagasta,
Dreamt up-country, to the weather
Of Chuqui Camata. Soon, at last,
They would come together,

Purple chasing yellow
Across the earth. . . .
They called it the rain shadow,
Brought it north

On honeymoon, around Cape Horn,
Through tango cities, African ports,
A past alive in a haunted future
Long before I was born—

A door banging in the wind,
A breakdown at the sound of trains,
A shuddering sob at the kitchen sink,
A window streaked with rain.

ESTACIÓN EL RETIRO, BUENOS AIRES

A run-down hall of echoes. Shout your name,
You will hear it again, from generations
Gone before you.... The souls they have become
By the million, look at them, transmigrating

Out of Europe, dragging sailors' trunks
Aboard the Pullmans—conscious of rank,
Edwardian.... There they go, to break the bank
Of the Gran Chaco, fornicate, die drunk

In an age of uprootings. One who flipped a coin
For South America, one evading War,
One who blew himself up, on the lonely floor
Of his own outstation. Dead, reborn

In the place of eternal return, is it any wonder
You hesitate, in thirty centigrade air,
A wilderness of shimmering track out there
Beyond the platforms, so many dead behind you,

Fathers and forefathers? Not to pass
Or live them through again at ticket-control,
The million immigrant lives that shoot like grass
Between the tracks — is praxis of the soul.

THE MYNAH BIRD

ELIZABETH BISHOP 1911–1979

Always pulling in
Alone, to some station
In the middle of nowhere,

Giving it a name,
Exactitudes. A glass
To be rubbed clean,

An unknown country seen
With the lonely eye
Of a spinster. Companions

There may be, and lovers,
But the mynah bird
In the hanging cage

On the platform, repeating
The unspeakable, passing along
The chatter of the ages

In transit, in their millions,
Neither here nor there,
Is your only heir.

BLOOR AND YONGE

There were flurries forecast
Out of the Arctic. And they came,
Touching my face
And were gone. Fingers of the dead

And the never-to-be-born,
Barely tangible, icily cold
At the instant of knowing.
I felt myself neither young nor old,

Neither son nor father,
Able to look both ways
As the lights changed, on Bloor and Yonge,
Two streets so infinitely long

My poles and tropics, Easts and Wests,
Could be held, simultanaeously,
In a single gaze.
Apparently weightless for once,

The forebears, the descendants
Relented, seeming to graze
Indigenous, in a time without cities,
A Canada of pure space

At every end, where the streets
Thinned out, and the ghosts about town.
I could walk straight through the traffic,
The snow would cut me down.

MERCATOR

He of the continents
Elongated, through the grid
Of latitude, longitude,

Dripping like honey
From a comb, to the hemisphere
Of slowed time

South of history.
Somebody once, in outer space,
Adjusted the light

And the earth changed colour,
Blushed. Bad conscience—
The bottom dropping out

Of power perspective,
Myth. The faces
In the changed mirror

Longer than they thought,
The fate of the body, drawn up,
A ladder into the attic

Of the mind, let down again
To wander, to graze
Through sub-millenial days,

The cycle of crops
And starvings, human knowledge
Grain by gleaner's grain.

SOMEWHERE

Somewhere a whole illiterate continent
Goes unnoticed, though there are people there too,
Real people, with humour, a point of view,
A dread of dying, a life of sentiment—

And you tell me there is nothing to write about!
Spare the language, spare yourself, my friend.
Join the external universe. Get out
Where the silence is too vast to comprehend

And words mean nothing. Everything will happen
With or without its signature, its tune.
A crop will bloom or fail. A drunk platoon

Rape villages, in the unreported zone
That poetry or journalism, open
Only to themselves, have never shown.

IN MEMORY OF

RYSZARD KAPUSCINSKI

1932–2007

Look for us, an Irishman, a Pole,
At the heart of Africa. Having fallen out
So long ago, with our own dark continent
Of Inquisitorial faith, Cartesian doubt.
Exiles, taking time out for the soul—
Our bleak outstation. Tired of argument
With the likes of myself, degenerate and sick,
A liberal tempter—Father Stanislawek

Would welcome one of his own. I see him now
So lonely, so delighted, on the run
Between river and kitchen, with a captured perch
In a bucket, a crate of bootleg beer
From Obasanjo barracks. As you know,

As you always knew, there is nothing here
But heat and people, years. A strawroofed church
Collapsed on itself, a Mary Immaculate nun

In bloodstained habit, on her nightly round.
Karl Marx and Alex Comfort, littered about
With Carlos Castaneda, on a dumping-ground
Of paperbacks, a midden of philosophies
Out behind the post-colonial house
I share with Jerzy. Thunderheads, months of drought—
The *coups d'etat* a thousand miles away
Are nothing to the power of everyday

Up-country, in the vast interior
Where the lives pass away, an after-image of cloud
On an old exposure. . . . Still, I'm happy here,
Not that I know it—home in the homeless crowd,
The anonymity. Put me in a wire
With Father Jerzy—*nothing to report.*
Not that you'll ever get here. Life is too short.
They are raising water in a rubber tyre

Tonight from a hole on main street. Hallelujah Jim
Is high in session. Charity, Patience, Grace,

Each with her smoke-ring and her tribe-marked face
Behind the wall, are belting out the hymns
In raucous antiphon. Lost on a map of becoming
Somewhere between the spirit-house and the stews,
Look for us outside space, in vacant time
Without history, who were never news.

OWENINY, UPPER REACHES

1

The sheepdogs flash, close in and disappear
In the rearview mirror. No, there is nothing here—

Or so they tell you, in the incestuous fug
Of Bellacorrick bar—from Nephin Beg

To the Belderg fields. Nothing for miles and miles.
So switch your engine off, be lost for a while,

Tune in to the skylark's high, unearthly stations,
Teach yourself humility and patience

That a day might pass, beneath Atlantic skies
And apperceptive light, through half-closed eyes—

The bog-cotton infinite, shimmering like a sea,
The gulls blown in on the wind, off Blacksod Bay,

The power station shut, the stock derailed
On rusty tracks. The obsolete, epic scale.

2

The mountain ash is lonely for the mountain.
Where there is no-one, let yourself be haunted.

Father, tapping Atacama wells,
Alone on a dried-up sea, with fossilised shells —

You in the Niger naked, decades later
Drunk on vastness, solitude, one lone bather —

Up the road, the unsung engineer
Of Bellacorrick, lonely, drunk out here —

Crowding in, the alcoholic ghosts,
Home to original homelessness, glad to be lost,

To find the empty space on the Mayo map,
To park the car in a blind spot, or a gap

In knowledge—exiled souls, self-haunted,
Mountain ash-trees, lonely for the mountain.

3

Only so far, they tell you. Here, the track
Fades out, and the river is a switchback

Of shallows, glides, and salmon spawning-redds
To the back of beyond. Pure watershed—

The arguments, the human cries torn off
In a crosswind, the tree grown through the roof

Of an abandoned house, where the cattle winter.
No-one comes through the door, they break and enter—

Long lost years.... And now, sweet smells of hay
On the other side of suffering, after a wet May

In a car already rusted, the tyres all blown,
Coming, on shattered fragments, into your own,

Crashed out, under travelling Irish skies,
Wondering is it here the waters rise.

Grateful acknowledgement is made to the editors of the following publications where these poems, or versions of them, first appeared: *Poetry Ireland Review*, *Poetry Review (London)*, *Poetry (Chicago)*, *Poetry London*, *The Warwick Review*, *Danish Journal of Irish Studies*, *Times Literary Supplement*, *The New Republic*, *The New Yorker*, *An tSionnach*, *Qualm*, *RTE radio*, *TG4 television*, *The Shop*, *Southword*, *Poetry Europe*, *Ploughshares*.